Parent's Introduction

We Both Read Books are delightful stories which **both** a parent **and** a child can participate in reading aloud. Developed in conjunction with early reading specialists, the books invite parents to read the more sophisticated text on the left-hand pages, while children are encouraged to read the right-hand pages, which have been specially written for beginning readers. The parent's text is preceded by a "talking parent" icon: ; the children's text is preceded by a "talking child" icon: .

Educators know that nothing helps children learn to read more than by reading aloud with their parents. However, the concentration necessary for reading is often difficult for young children. That is why *We Both Read Books* offer short periods of reading by the child, alternating with periods of being read to by their parent. The result is a much more enjoyable and enriching experience for both!

Most of the words used in the child's text should be familiar to them. Others can easily be sounded out. An occasional difficult word will often be first introduced in the parent's text, distinguished with **bold lettering**. Pointing out these words, as you read them, will help familiarize them to your child. You may also find it helpful to read the entire book to your child the first time, then invite them to participate on the second reading.

We hope that both you and your children enjoy the *We Both Read Books* and that they will help start your children off on a lifetime of reading enjoyment!

We Both Read: Jack and the Beanstalk

———————————————

We Both Read® is a registered trademark of Treasure Bay, Inc.

Published by Treasure Bay, Inc.
40 Sir Francis Drake Blvd.
San Anselmo, CA 94960 USA

PRINTED IN SINGAPORE

Library of Congress Catalog Card Number: 97-62023
Hardcover ISBN: 1-891327-00-3
Paperback ISBN: 1-891327-15-1

05 06 07 08 09 / 10 9 8 7 6 5 4 3 2

We Both Read® Books
Patent No. 5,957,693

Visit us online at:
www.webothread.com

WE BOTH READ™

Jack
and the
Beanstalk

Adapted by Sindy McKay

Illustrated by Lydia Halverson

TREASURE BAY

Once upon a time a poor widow lived in a tiny cottage with her young son Jack. Jack was a good boy, but he knew nothing of the world beyond his home.

Jack and his mother were so poor that the only thing they had to eat or drink was milk from their cow. One day the cow stopped giving milk, leaving **Jack** and his mother with nothing at all to fill their bellies.

Mother gave Jack the cow.

She told Jack to take it to town.

She told Jack to sell it.

Jack did as he was told.

Jack set off to town and had not traveled far when a woman approached and said, "Good morning, Jack."

"Good morning," he replied, surprised that she knew his name.

"That's a fine looking cow," said the woman. "I will trade you four **beans** for it."

Jack looked up at his big cow.

He looked down at the small beans.

He said to the woman,

"No, thank you."

"You drive a hard bargain, Jack," the woman replied, "but I want that cow. So I will give you five beans for it." Then the woman whispered in his ear. "These are no ordinary beans, Jack. They are magic. They hold the answer to all your **dreams**."

Jack had many dreams.

He wanted to see his mother happy.

So he gave the woman his cow.

Then he took the beans to his mother.

But his mother was *not* happy.

Jack told his mother the beans were magic, but she did not believe in magic anymore. She threw the beans out the window, then sent Jack to bed with an empty stomach.

The next morning she was surprised to find a great tall **beanstalk** had grown outside their window. But Jack was not surprised at all.

Jack kissed his mother good-bye.
Then he went up the beanstalk
to find his dreams.

When Jack got to the top,
he saw a very big house.

As Jack walked toward the big house, he was once again met by the woman who had traded him the magic beans. She told him that a horrible **giant** lived in the house. And that when Jack was very young, this very same **giant** had killed Jack's father and stolen all he owned.

"So you see, Jack, everything in that house really belongs to you and your mother."

Jack knew what he had to do.

He had to get his things back.

He had to get them for his mother.

He had to get them
from the big, mean giant!

As Jack neared the huge house, he spotted the giant's wife sweeping the doorstep. Jack was **scared**. He knew that little boys were a favorite meal of both giants and giantesses alike, so he did not ask to be invited in. Instead he grabbed her broom and was swept through the door.

Everything in the house was very big.

It made Jack feel very small.

It also made him feel very scared.

He did not want to meet the giant.

Suddenly Jack heard the sound of enormous footsteps! He scurried up a curtain cord to a high shelf where he quickly hid inside a sack of gold! Then he heard the giant shout;

" Fee-fi-fo-fum
I smell the blood of an Englishman!
Be he alive, or be he dead
I'll grind his bones to make my bread!"

The giant came into the room.

He was very big and very mean.

The room shook with each step he took.

The giant began to tear the room apart, looking for Jack. His wife, upon hearing he was looking for a yummy little boy, eagerly joined in. But soon the giant grew tired of looking and ordered his wife to bring him his **sacks** of **gold** instead.

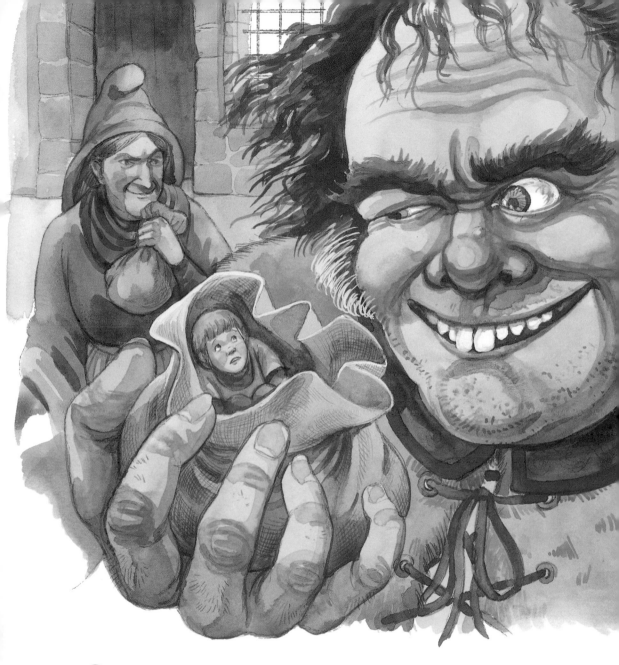

The giant took the sack that Jack was in.
But he did not open it.

The giant took another sack
and began to count his gold.

Fortunately the giant was not very good with numbers and had to keep starting over with "1." This tired him quickly and soon he fell asleep.

That's when Jack tiptoed from his hiding place to stare in awe at the giant's gold (which really belonged to him and his mother).

Jack knew what he had to do.

He had to get his gold back.

He had to get it for his mother.

He had to get it from the big, mean giant!

Jack hoisted a sack of gold upon his back. Then, so the giant would not think it missing when he awoke, Jack replaced the gold with a sack of beans.

Quiet as a mouse, Jack slipped out of the giant's house, then ran all the way to the beanstalk and quickly slid back down to earth!

Jack's mother was very happy
to see Jack and the gold.
But she did not want Jack to ever
go back up the beanstalk!

But Jack knew what he had to do.

Several days later, Jack climbed up the beanstalk once more. He ran straight to the giant's house and heaved a huge rock at the big front door. When the giant's wife opened it to see who was knocking, Jack slipped into the house behind her.

Jack went from room to room.

He saw many things.

Things the giant took from his father.

And then the house began to shake!

The giant was home!

" Fee-fi-fo-fum
  I smell the blood of an Englishman!
  Be he alive, or be he dead
  I'll grind his bones to make my bread!"

Jack gasped in fear as he crouched behind a nearby cage to hide. From there he watched in terror as the giant and his **wife** tore the room apart looking for him.

Jack sat very still.

He did not make a sound.

Soon the giant got tired of looking.

He and his wife gave up.

The giant ordered his wife to bring him his cage with the golden **goose** — the very cage behind which Jack was hiding.

Jack scampered into the shadows and continued to watch as the giant took the **goose** from its cage.

What Jack saw next nearly took his breath away! For the golden goose began to lay golden eggs!

Jack knew what he had to do.

He had to get his goose back.

He had to get it for his mother.

He had to get it from the big, mean giant!

The giant soon grew tired of watching the wondrous goose lay golden eggs and, with a yawn and stretch, he fell asleep.

That's when Jack tiptoed from his hiding place and grabbed the golden goose. Then, to keep it from honking, Jack snatched a chunk of bread and fed it to the goose as he fled.

Jack ran out the door.

He ran down the road.

Then the goose went "honk!"
and woke the giant up.

The giant leapt from his chair to chase Jack, his huge strides
bringing him closer with every step! Jack jumped onto the
beanstalk just as the big mean giant reached out his arm to
grab him!

Luckily for Jack, the giant missed.

Jack went down the beanstalk.

His mother was at the bottom.

She was glad that Jack was safe.

She did not want Jack to ever go back up.

But Jack knew what he had to do.

The next time Jack returned to the giant's big house, he sneaked in through an open window.

Once inside, Jack heard a haunting voice singing a beautiful song. He followed the sound and found the giant listening to a magic **harp**.

Jack knew what he had to do.
He had to get the harp back.
He had to get it for his mother.

He had to get it from the big,
mean giant!

Suddenly the giant ordered the harp to stop singing and he put his nose into the air to sniff. Jack froze. He knew what was coming next …

"Fee-fi-fo-fum
  I smell the blood of an Englishman!
  Be he alive, or be he dead
  I'll grind his bones to make my bread!"

The giant looked for Jack.

His wife looked for Jack.

But soon they got tired and gave up.

The giant ordered the harp to sing again and this time she sang a lullaby. Before long the rafters were shaking with the giant's mighty snores.

That's when Jack tiptoed from his hiding place and grabbed up the magic harp. Then, to keep the giant from chasing him, he hid the giant's shoes inside a cooking pot.

Jack ran out the door.
He ran down the road.

Then the harp began to sing
and woke the giant up!

The furious giant jumped up to chase Jack! Immediately he realized that his shoes were missing. This only made him even more angry – and more determined than ever to catch Jack and gobble him up!

The giant frantically searched for his missing shoes, then finally gave up and chased after Jack in his bare feet!

Jack ran very fast.
But the giant ran faster!

Jack went down the beanstalk.
But the giant went down the
beanstalk, too!

Jack slid down that beanstalk in the wink of an eye, then he shouted for his mother to bring him an ax.

With three mighty whacks, Jack chopped that beanstalk down. The plant toppled and crashed down to earth! And with it crashed the big mean giant!

That was the end of the beanstalk.
That was the end of the giant, too.

And Jack and his mother lived
happily ever after.

⌐ *The End* ⌐

If you liked *Jack and the Beanstalk*, here is another
We Both Read® Book you are sure to enjoy!

In this delightfully funny version of the classic story,
a princess makes promises to a frog, who finds the
golden ball she lost in a pond. Once she has her ball
back, the princess has no interest in keeping her
promises to the frog and she runs back to the castle.
Much to her surprise, the frog comes knocking at the
castle door, looking for the princess and all that she
promised.